Who Pooped in the Park?

written by Gary D. Robson • illustrated by Elijah Brady Clark

FARCOUNTRY
PRESS

To my brother, Bill, who told me repeatedly that I
had talent and could do anything I wanted to do.
Now, I'm doing it. Thanks for believing in me.

ISBN: 978-1-56037-318-6

© 2005 by Farcountry Press
Text © 2005 by Gary D. Robson
Illustrations © 2005 by Farcountry Press

Who Pooped in the Park? is a registered trademark of
Farcountry Press.

For more information about our books, write
Farcountry Press, P.O. Box 5630, Helena, MT 59604;
call (800) 821-3874; or visit www.farcountrypress.com.

Manufactured by:
Bang Printing
3323 Oak Street
Brainerd, MN 56401
in March 2017

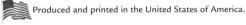 Produced and printed in the United States of America.

21 20 19 18 17   5 6 7 8 9

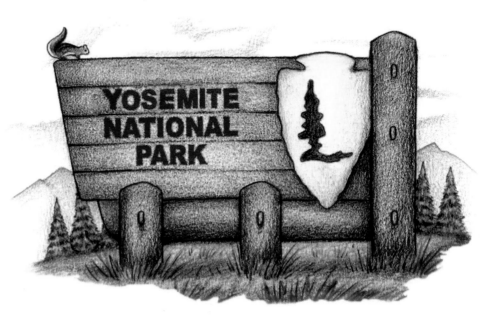

"Dad? I have to go to the bathroom." Michael squirmed in the back seat.

"We'll be at our campground in just half an hour," said Dad. "We're in Yosemite National Park now."

"He's just nervous," said Michael's sister. "He thinks a bear's gonna eat him." She growled at Michael and made her fingers look like claws.

"Stop it, Emily," said Mom. "Nobody is getting eaten by anything."

Michael was very excited about the trip, but Emily was right. He *was* nervous. He had just read a book about bears. He knew how big they could get, especially grizzly bears. And he was afraid that a hungry bear would eat just about anything—maybe even a boy.

"I *am* kind of scared of grizzly bears," admitted Michael.

"Don't worry," Dad told him. "There aren't any grizzlies in California anymore. Just black bears. And we'll show you how to count a black bear's toes and never get close enough to be scared."

"Here's our campsite. Let's set up the tent. Then we can go for a walk and I'll show you what I mean," Dad said. Michael was awfully worried about bear toes, but tried not to show it.

"Let's hurry!" said Emily. "I want to see some animals!"

Once the tent was up, the whole family went for a hike. Emily started to complain before they even left the campground. "I haven't seen any animals yet. Maybe there aren't any here!"

Mule Deer

Mountain Lion

Gray Owl

"Sure there are," said Dad. "Let's see what we can learn about them from their sign."

"Sign?" said Michael. "You mean like a sign at the zoo?"

"I'm talking about signs that the animal has been around. See these holes in the ground with the pathways around them? Those are entrances to ground squirrel burrows." Dad explained.

"Check out the tracks by this burrow!" said Michael.

"Yes," said Mom. "Those are ground squirrel tracks."

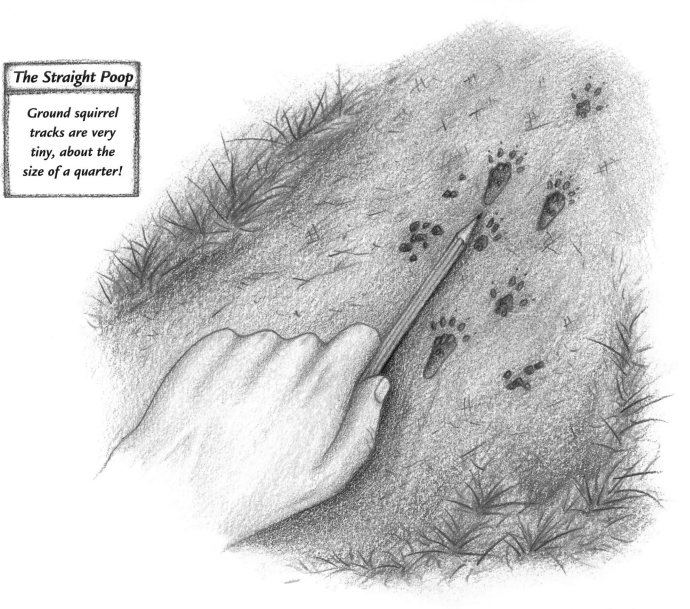

"Look at how far the claw marks are from the little toes. They have long claws for their size."

"And here's some ground squirrel scat, too," added Dad.

"Scat?" asked Emily, looking a little less grumpy. "What's scat?"

"It's the word hikers and trackers use for animal poop," Dad replied.

"See, Michael," said Dad. "We don't have to get up close to an animal to learn about it. Instead of a close encounter of the *scary* kind, we'll have a close encounter of the *poopy* kind."

Everybody laughed, and Mom made a gross-out face.

"Dad! Mom! Look over here! I found bunny scat!" yelled Michael. "It's just like what we have in Fluffy's cage."

"We came all the way to Yosemite National Park for *that*?" grumbled Emily. "Michael's bunny makes plenty of poop at home."

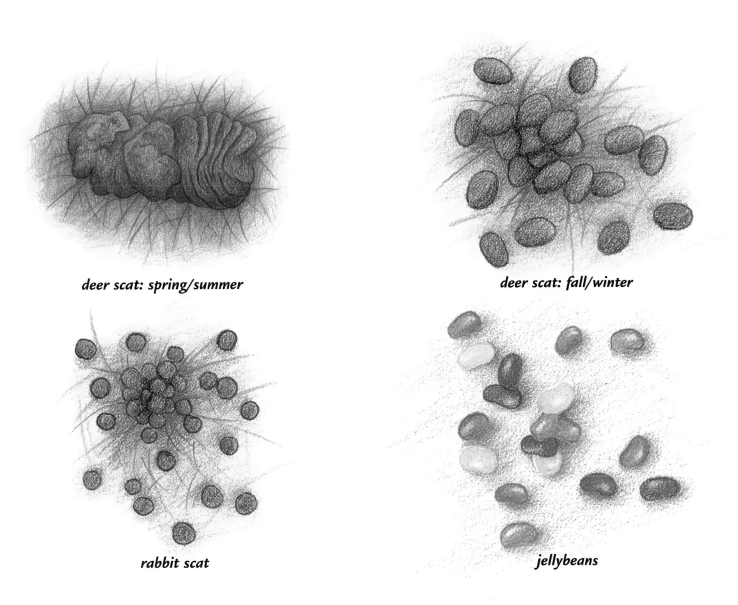

deer scat: spring/summer

deer scat: fall/winter

rabbit scat

jellybeans

"That's not from a rabbit," said Mom. "It's from a deer."

"Right! Bunny poop looks like little round balls," added Dad. "Deer scat is shaped more like jellybeans."

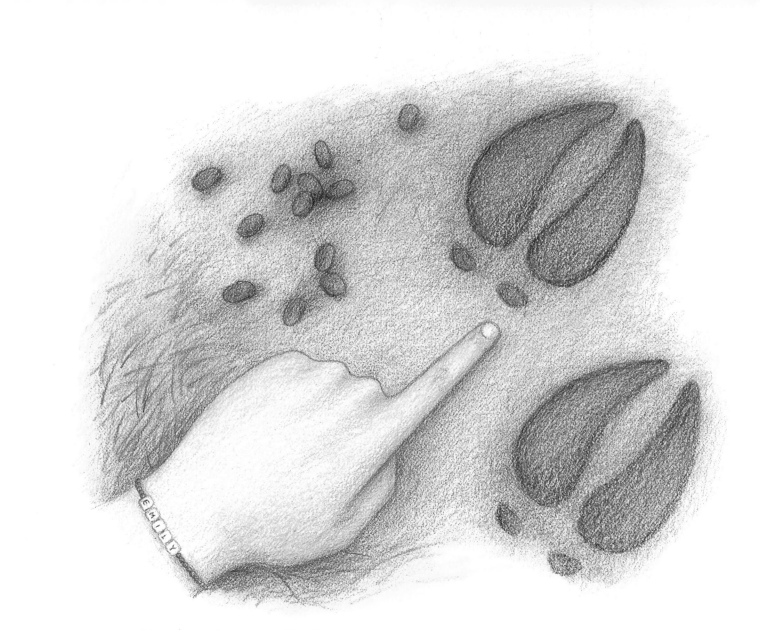

"Are these deer tracks?" Michael asked.

"Yes!" said Mom. "See how they're split? They have hooves with two parts."

"What are these marks?" asked Emily. She was starting to get interested.

dew claw

hoof

"Those are from its dew claws," said Mom. "They're little claws behind the hooves. Dew claws sometimes show in deer tracks in soft ground. Lots of other animals have dew claws, too, including cats and dogs."

"Oh, no!" said Michael. "Here's one of his antlers. Did a bear eat him?" Michael looked around nervously.

Dad bent down by the antler. "No, he's fine. Deer shed their antlers every winter and then grow a new, bigger set the next year."

18

"This deer was in a hurry, though," said Mom, as she studied the ground.

Michael and Emily went over to look.

"How can you tell?" said Michael.

The Straight Poop

Sometimes mule deer bounce along with all four feet hitting the ground together. This is called "stotting" or "pronking."

stotting
or
pronking

galloping

walking

"The hoofprints get very far apart here," Mom explained, "and the back prints are in front of the front prints."

"It was walking backwards?" said Emily.

"No, this deer was galloping. Something scared it and it was moving fast."

"I know what scared the deer," Dad called.

The family hurried over to look.

"This is coyote scat," Dad said, "and there are coyote tracks all around here."

"They look like dog tracks," said Michael.

"That's because coyotes are members of the dog family," explained Dad.

"There were a lot of coyotes around here," said Mom. "See how the adults left big tracks and the pups left smaller ones?"

"Their den is probably nearby. I'll bet they scared the deer away," Dad guessed.

"Did the coyotes get him?" Michael asked.

"I don't think so," said Mom. "Look!"

Far across the meadow, they saw a family of coyotes, lying in the sun.

As they walked along the trail into the woods, Michael looked all over for tracks.

"Look, everyone! I found another coyote track."

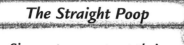

The Straight Poop

Since cats can retract their claws, their tracks don't show claw marks. The only dog that doesn't show claw marks is a gray fox. Their claws are so small and sharp that they can climb trees like a cat.

coyote track

mountain lion track

"That's not a coyote track," said Dad. "It doesn't show any claw marks, and the front of the big pad looks dented in."

"It's too big to be a bobcat track, so I'd say it's from a mountain lion," said Mom.

"Are they as big as panthers?" Michael asked, wide-eyed.

"Actually, that's another name for the same cat," Mom said with a smile. "Mountain lion, cougar, panther, painter, puma, and catamount are all names for the same animal!"

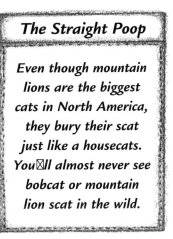

The Straight Poop

Even though mountain lions are the biggest cats in North America, they bury their scat just like a housecats. You⊠ll almost never see bobcat or mountain lion scat in the wild.

mountain lion

bobcat

"Wow! There's a huge pile of scat right here in the middle of the trail," called Michael. "Is it from a mountain lion?"

"This scat couldn't have come from a meat eater like a mountain lion. It looks like it has grass and oats in it," said Dad.

"It's horse poop!" said Emily.

"Right," said Mom. "People ride horses out here. See if you can find any tracks."

The Straight Poop

Horses walk while they poop, but they stop and stand still to pee.

deer hoof

horse hoof

The Straight Poop

Special metal shoes are attached to horses' hooves to protect them from wear. These shoes appear in the tracks horses leave behind.

horse hoof with metal shoe
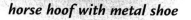

Emily found tracks, all right, but they didn't look like she expected.

"That's an awfully funny-shaped hoof," she said.

"Horses don't have split hooves like bison and deer," said Dad. "There's just one part."

"What are these white streaks on the rocks over here?" asked Michael.

"That's called guano," said Dad.

"I know what that is!" exclaimed Emily. "We learned about it in school. Guano is bat poop!"

"Right," said Dad. "Here in Yosemite National Park you can find the biggest bats in North America. They're called spotted bats."

The Straight Poop

Spotted bats use sonar to find bugs. The bats make high-pitched squeaks, which bounce off insects and tell them where their next meal is!

"Do they suck blood like vampires?" said Michael with a shudder.

"No, they eat bugs," said Dad. "There are no vampire bats around here."

"Is this more bat poop?" said Michael, looking at a tree.

"No," said Mom. "It's from an owl. See these tracks with two toes pointing forward and two pointing back, and the owl pellets around the base of the tree?"

34

The Straight Poop

Owls eat all kinds
of small animals,
including lizards
and birds; mice
and other rodents
are favorites.

"Owl pellets?" said Emily.

"Owls eat their prey whole," explained Mom. "The parts they can't digest,
like hair and bones, get coughed up in a pellet like this."

"Yuck!" said Emily.

"You can tell this was a big owl by the size of the tracks and the pellets," said Mom. "The bigger the owl, the bigger the owl pellets."

"There are a bunch of different owls in Yosemite National Park," said Dad. "My favorite is the great grey owl."

"There sure are a lot of bats and birds around here," Emily said.

"Yosemite National Park has 17 types of bats and over 200 types of birds," said Mom. "If we're lucky, we might see our national bird, the bald eagle!"

"Whoa, Dad! What happened to this tree? Did another porcupine do that?"

"Something was sharpening its claws, Michael, not eating the bark. And if you look how high those scratch marks go, it was pretty big!"

"It's not just the animal that's big," said Emily. "Look at the size of this poop!"

"It looks like we found your black bear," said Dad. "Let's see what you learned today. What can you figure out about this bear?"

"It's probably as tall as you, and it has really long claws," said Michael.

"I don't see any hair or bones in the poop," said Emily, "so it must have been eating plants."

"Good!" Mom said. "What else?"

The Straight Poop

Black bears eat almost anything. They mostly live on leaves, nuts, berries, insects, twigs, and honey, but they also hunt small animals and fish.

"Here's its footprint," said Michael. "It's really big, and it has more toes than a coyote or mountain lion."

"I told you you'd be able to count a black bear's toes," laughed Dad.

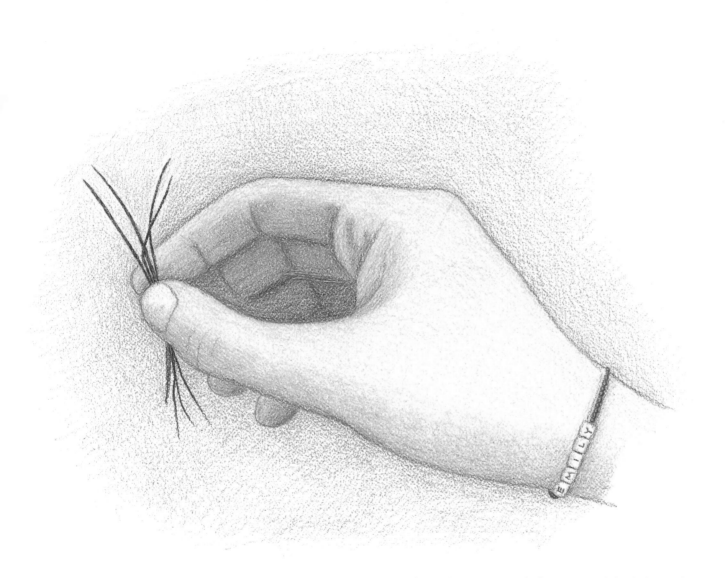

"It rubbed off some hair on the tree," said Emily. "You said this was a black bear, but these hairs are reddish brown."

"Black bears come in a bunch of different colors," explained Mom. "They can be black, brown, or cinnamon-colored, like this one. Some of them are almost white."

As they ate dinner that night, everyone talked about how much fun they had.

"We didn't see very many animals," said Emily, "but it seemed like we did."

"And I didn't get scared once," said Michael.

Tracks and Scat Notes

Black Bear
Large tracks showing five toes and claws. Scat changes depending on diet but usually contains vegetation.

Bobcat
Tracks are very similar to a mountain lion's, but about half the size. Scat is usually buried.

Coyote
Tracks are like a dog's, with four toes, and show visible claw marks. Scat is very dark in color with tapered ends and usually contains hair.

Great Grey Owl
Tracks show four toes: two pointing forward and two pointing back or sideways. Scat is runny and white. "Cough pellets" or "owl pellets" contain fur and bones.

Ground Squirrel
Front track shows four toes and back track shows five. Scat is smaller than rabbit scat, and not as round.

Tracks and Scat Notes

Horse
Tracks are much bigger than deer tracks and are not split. Scat is in chunks, with roughage from vegetation often visible.

Mountain Lion
Tracks are bigger than a coyote's, but claws don't show. Scat is rarely seen because they bury it.

Mule Deer
Pointy split-hoof tracks. Scat is long and oval-shaped like jellybeans, not round like a rabbit's.

Spotted Bat
Bats rarely land on soft ground to leave tracks. Scat is runny and white.

The Author

Gary Robson lives in Montana, not far from Yellowstone National Park. He has written dozens of books and hundreds of articles, mostly related to science, nature, and technology. www.GaryDRobson.com

The Illustrator

Elijah Brady Clark has been passionate about design and illustration for as long as he can remember. After living his dream of traveling the United States in an Airstream Bambi Travel Trailer, he returned to northwestern Montana's Flathead Valley, where he grew up. He currently works as a designer and illustrator.

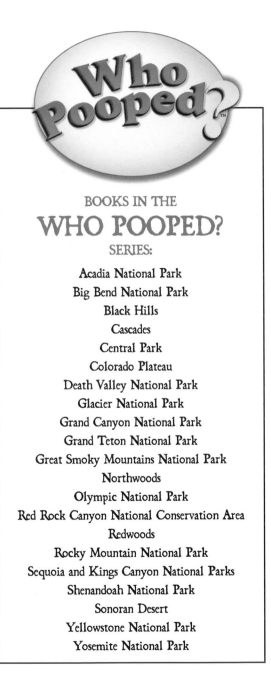

Who Pooped?

BOOKS IN THE
WHO POOPED?
SERIES:

Acadia National Park
Big Bend National Park
Black Hills
Cascades
Central Park
Colorado Plateau
Death Valley National Park
Glacier National Park
Grand Canyon National Park
Grand Teton National Park
Great Smoky Mountains National Park
Northwoods
Olympic National Park
Red Rock Canyon National Conservation Area
Redwoods
Rocky Mountain National Park
Sequoia and Kings Canyon National Parks
Shenandoah National Park
Sonoran Desert
Yellowstone National Park
Yosemite National Park